How Toys

Wheels and Axles

Siân Smith

www.raintreepublishers.co.uk
Visit our website to find out more information about Raintree books.

To order:
☎ Phone 0845 6044371
🖹 Fax +44 (0) 1865 312263
💻 Email myorders@raintreepublishers.co.uk

Customers from outside the UK please telephone +44 1865 312262

Raintree is an imprint of Capstone Global Library Limited, a company incorporated in England and Wales having its registered office at 7 Pilgrim Street, London, EC4V 6LB – Registered company number: 6695582

Text © Capstone Global Library Limited 2013
First published in hardback in 2013
First published in paperback in 2014
The moral rights of the proprietor have been asserted.

Edited by Dan Nunn, Rebecca Rissman, and Sian Smith
Designed by Joanna Hinton-Malivoire
Picture research by Mica Brancic
Production by Victoria Fitzgerald
Originated by Capstone Global Library Ltd
Printed in China

ISBN 978 1 4062 3803 7 (hardback)
16 15 14 13 12
10 9 8 7 6 5 4 3 2 1

ISBN 978 1 4062 3810 5 (paperback)
16 15 14 13
10 9 8 7 6 5 4 3 2 1

British Library Cataloguing in Publication Data
Smith, Sian.
 Wheels and axles. -- (How toys work)
 1. Wheels--Juvenile literature. 2. Axles--Juvenile
 literature.
 I. Title II. Series
 621.8'11-dc22

Acknowledgements
The author and publisher are grateful to the following for permission to reproduce copyright material: © Capstone Global Library Ltd pp.7 (Tudor Photography), 11 bottom (Lord and Leverett); © Capstone Publishers pp.5, 8, 9, 18, 12 inset, 12 main, 13 inset, 13 main, 23 top (Karon Dubke); Shutterstock pp. 4 bottom left (© Kellis), 4 bottom right (© Studio Smart), 4 top left (© Mikeledray), 4 top right (© Jamalludin), 6 (© Zurijeta), 10 bottom (© Martin Allinger), 10 top (© charles taylor), 11 top (© Oriori), 15 (© Mika Heittola), 16 (© Alexander Sakhatovsky), 17 (© Pixel1962), 19 (© Greenland), 20 (© Losevsky Pavel), 21 (© Rupena), 22a (© Martin Plsek), 22b (© Vlue), 22d (© Chepe Nicoli), 22d (© Jakub Krechowicz), 23 bottom (© Alexander Sakhatovsky).

Cover photograph of a boy on a bicycle reproduced with permission of Getty Images (altrendo images/Altrendo). Back cover photograph of a scooter reproduced with permission of Shutterstock (© Greenland).

We would like to thank David Harrison, Nancy Harris, Dee Reid, and Diana Bentley for their assistance in the preparation of this book.

Every effort has been made to contact copyright holders of material reproduced in this book. Any omissions will be rectified in subsequent printings if notice is given to the publisher.

Contents

Different toys

There are many different kinds
of toys.

Toys work in different ways.

Wheels

wheel

Some toys move on wheels.

A go-cart moves on wheels.

Toys move when they are pushed
or pulled.

Toys with wheels are easier to move.

metal

plastic

Toy wheels can be made of metal or plastic.

wood

rubber

Toy wheels can be made of wood or rubber.

Axles

axle

An axle is like a rod.

axle

Some axles stay still. Wheels move around on them.

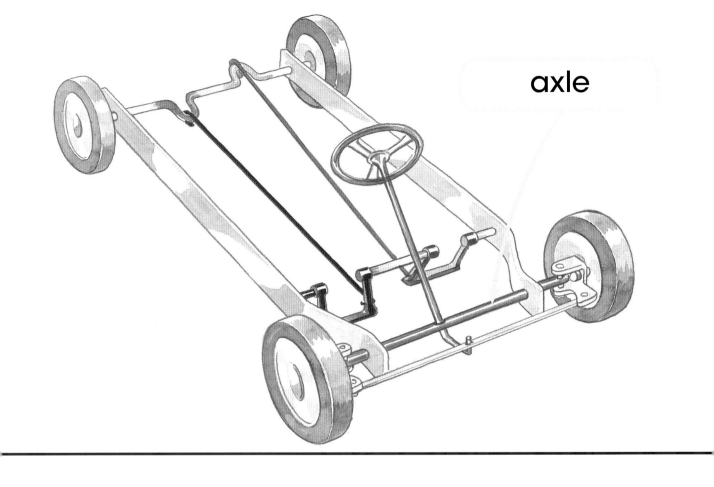

axle

Some wheels are stuck on axles.

When the axle moves, the wheels move too.

Moving toys

Electricity can make some things move.

Electricity makes the wheels on this racing car move.

Water makes some toy wheels move.

Pushes from people make some toy wheels move.

A roundabout is a wheel you can push.

Roller skates have wheels you
can push.

Quiz

Which one of these toys is missing its wheels?

Answer on page 24

Picture glossary

 **axle** a rod which has a wheel at each end

 **electricity** electricity can be used to make some things move. There is a small amount of electricity in batteries.

Index

Answer to question on page 22: Toy d is missing its wheels.

Notes for parents and teachers

Introduction

Show the children a collection of toys. One or more of the toys should have wheels. Ask the children if they can spot the toy or toys with wheels. Do they know what an axle is? Why do we use wheels?

More information about wheels and axles

Explain that we use wheels to make things easier to move. You could demonstrate this by pushing a toy car with wheels, and one without. Show the children a good example of two wheels on an axle. Explain that an axle is like a bar or rod, and a wheel is put on each end of the axle. Some axles are fixed in place and the wheels are free to move around on them. Some axles are free to move but the wheels are fixed in place, then when the axle turns or moves, the wheels move too.

Follow up activities

Tell the children that there are five wheels on page 14. Can they see the fifth wheel? Explain that a steering wheel is an example of a wheel on an axle, too. Ask the children to sort toys or pictures of toys based on the type of material the toy wheels are made from. For more advanced work on simple machines, children can work with an adult to discuss and play the games at: www.edheads.org/activities/simple-machines

24